STUNT PERFORMERS

IN ACTION

BY ALEX MONNIG

Published by The Child's World®
1980 Lookout Drive • Mankato, MN 56003-1705
800-599-READ • www.childsworld.com

ISBN 9781503816336

LCCN 2016945640

Printed in the United States of America
PA02320

TABLE OF
CONTENTS

FAST FACTS

What's the Job?

- Stunt performers are people who are paid to perform amazing, dangerous feats.

- Stunt performers are used in many movies and TV shows. They appear in action sequences that could put other actors at risk.

- Stunt performers often hone their skills at training centers, such as the International Stunt School.

The Dangers

- Stunt performers put themselves at risk every time they perform. They often jump from great heights or work with dangerous weapons.

- Stunt performance can be a difficult career. Workers are usually hired for only one show or movie. When that job is over, a stunt performer must search for more work.

Important Stats

- There are approximately 59,000 stunt performers employed in the United States.

- Stunt performers earn approximately $900 a day. A weekly rate is approximately $3,378.

Chapter 1

HAL NEEDHAM'S HORSE COLLARING

The buzz of the airplane's engine filled Hal Needham's ears. His eyes were watery. The wind whipped across his face. He was on the back of a flying Cessna 150 plane.

Most people would find this action crazy. For Hal, it was work. The year was 1950, and Hal had been hired for a TV show called *You Asked for It*. For his stunt scene, he had to hang from a moving airplane, jump off, and tackle a man riding a horse.

Hal's feet were planted on the rear right landing wheels of the plane. His hands tightly gripped a pole attached to the right wing of the plane. Hal knew many things could go wrong. One small slip could send him tumbling to the ground. Or the pilot could crash the plane. Hal had no protection if they crashed. Even if Hal made the jump to the ground, he could land awkwardly and break a limb. Even worse, he could break his neck.

◄ **Hal Needham performed many stunts involving horses.**

The plane started to catch up to the horse. The plane reached speeds of 58 miles per hour (93 km/h). It was only 16 feet (4.9 m) off the ground. The pilot had to point the nose of the plane higher up than normal to keep it flying. The low height was not the only challenge. The pilot could not see the horse on the ground. So Hal had to guide him with hand gestures.

Hal's mind was racing. He was guiding the pilot. He was holding on for his life. And he was trying to figure out when to make his move. He knew he would have to jump 15 to 20 feet (4.6 to 6.1 m) to reach the rider on horseback. Then Hal had to be sure to make contact with the rider so that the tackle looked real. He also had to avoid hitting the heavy horse. Hal was most worried that the animal might fall on both men.

Hal waited for the perfect moment. Then he leaped, flying through the air. Soaring toward the ground, Hal wrapped his arms around the rider's midsection. Both men tumbled to the ground and rolled. Dust kicked up around them. The horse kept going, trying to race the airplane.

The stunt was a success! Hal and the rider were thrilled. But the show's director was not. The actors had performed the stunt far away from the camera. The action was not in focus. So Hal, the pilot, and the rider had to risk injury all over again. Luckily, they nailed it on the second take.

Hal appeared in approximately 300 movies and 4,500 TV episodes during his long career. The art of being a stunt performer has changed since Hal's time. But the courage and skill needed to perform crazy feats is still in demand.

▲ **Hal Needham received an award for the great stunts he performed during his career.**

Chapter 2

SHAUNA DUGGINS DIGS DEEP

Stunt performer Shauna Duggins pushed the gas pedal to the floor and launched her car into a lake. The car slammed into the water's surface and started to sink. The stunt was going according to plan. But then something went wrong.

The impact from hitting the water sealed the car's doors and windows shut. Shauna was trapped. She thought she was sinking to her death, 20 feet (6 m) below the surface. But then Shauna calmed herself. She had planned for the worst. Being a stunt performer requires lots of planning.

Shauna wrapped her hands tightly around the steering wheel. She used it as a **fulcrum** for her body. She used all her strength and her full body weight to push against the car door. The seal started to break. Shauna kept pushing. This was a life-or-death situation.

◄ Stunt performers risk drowning when they attempt stunts in the water.

Finally the door opened. Shauna swam up to the surface and burst through the water. A sense of relief washed over her. None of the crewmembers even knew she had been in danger.

Stunt performers know their safety is at risk every time they perform. They also know that preparation helps decrease the chance of disaster. Shauna and other stunt performers put their trust in **stunt coordinators**. They also trust each other.

Shauna learned this firsthand when she was a **stunt double** on the movie *Charlie's Angels*. She was in a fight scene with Donna Evans, another stunt performer. The suit Shauna had to wear in the scene was skintight with no room for padding. It could not protect her from being thrown down a set of stairs, which was what the scene required.

Shauna and Donna wanted to get the best shot possible. Donna suggested that they roll down the stone stairs together, and Shauna agreed. The women went to work coming up with a plan. Donna knew she could not get a good grip on Shauna's suit. Instead, Shauna would hold on to Donna to keep the two performers in control of the fall.

The director yelled action. The women burst through a set of doors at the top of the stairs and began their tumble. Their legs flew around as they rolled over each other. Their bodies slammed repeatedly on the cold, hard stairs.

The director yelled cut, and Shauna lay motionless at the bottom of the stairs. Donna feared the worst. She thought Shauna had hit her head and suffered a brutal injury. But Shauna was fine. Luckily, the only thing that was injured was her pride. Her costume had split open in the back!

▲ Falling down stairs can be a dangerous stunt when the performer is not wearing a helmet.

Chapter 3

JACKIE CHAN DOES IT HIMSELF

Jackie Chan had one chance to perform the stunt perfectly. He also had a great chance of dying.

Jackie mentally prepared himself. It was 1985, and he was making a movie called *Police Story*. The movie was being filmed in a shopping mall. The scene called for Jackie to leap from a railing and grab a pole. The top of the pole was approximately 100 feet (30 m) off the ground. And the pole was covered in glass lights. After sliding down the pole, Jackie would crash through glass and wood and onto the marble floor.

Fans loved Jackie's frantic fight scenes. And he loved putting his body on the line for incredible action sequences. But right now, all Jackie could do was hope he would be all right.

The movie cameras rolled. **Extras** on set watched nervously. Jackie looked down, and then he hopped up on the railing.

◀ Jackie Chan, who began his career in Hong Kong, has made many movies in the United States.

He squatted and held it with both hands. His moment was now or never.

Jackie shifted his weight back. Then he pushed off toward the metal pole. He grabbed it with both hands and wrapped his legs around it. Almost instantly, bulbs started to shatter and burst. Shards of glass flew everywhere.

Jackie held on to the pole for dear life. The **friction** of the pole felt like fire as he spun down it. Jackie's hands seared, giving him second-degree burns. But if he let go, he would risk death.

Glass shards and intense heat were not his only concerns. The pole's end was higher than the floor. Jackie knew the fall would be painful. All he could do was position himself appropriately and hope the fall didn't hurt too much.

Jackie straightened his legs outward, almost as if he was sitting on the floor. Then he let go of the pole. He burst through the glass on his way to the ground. His backside caused the glass to explode into tiny pieces. Jackie slammed to the floor. The stunt was over. But the scene was not. Jackie immediately got up and chased his target to complete the scene.

Jackie had survived. But he was in bad shape. In addition to the burns on his hands, he had a back injury. He had also dislocated his pelvis, which nearly paralyzed him.

Jackie went on to do hundreds more stunts in dozens of movies. But in 2012, he decided to use **green screen** technology and stunt doubles. Jackie had suffered dozens of breaks, bruises, dislocations, and cuts in his career. So he figured it was time to stop tempting fate.

▲ **Stunt performers often use safety ropes that are removed with special effects.**

Chapter 4

NIK WALLENDA'S WILD WALK

Nik Wallenda looked down at the crashing, foaming water 121 feet (37 m) below him. A heavy mist hung around him. Nik focused. He knew he would need laser-like concentration to complete his tightrope walk across Niagara Falls.

The year was 2012, and Nik was trying to make history. The Niagara Gorge is approximately 7 miles (11 km) long. Nobody had walked over it for 116 years. The waterfalls sit at the beginning of the gorge. Nobody had ever walked directly over the falls.

Nik was no stranger to dangerous stunts. He was part of the Flying Wallendas family. His uncles and grandfathers had completed dozens of amazing stunts.

Because Nik's walk was a TV special, it was safer than a typical tightrope walk. Broadcaster ABC made him wear a harness. But many things could still go wrong, and Nik knew it.

◀ Nik carried a balancing bar as he walked across Niagara Falls.

Nik crept toward the cliff's edge where the beginning of the cable sat. He would be walking on the single cable. The cable was 1,800 feet (550 m) long and just two inches (5 cm) wide. It stretched across Niagara Falls from the United States into Canada.

The time had come for Nik to achieve something he had dreamed of nearly all his life. He stepped onto the cable. After all the preparation, it was showtime.

The black night sky surrounded him. So did heavy, swirling wind. The wind bashed him from the front and hit him from the sides.

Nik needed to focus and put one foot in front of the other. But the loud waves continued to crash below. Thick, moist air from the falls got in his eyes. Nik had prepared for this. But no amount of training compares to the actual stunt.

He fought through the elements. Near the midway point of his walk, he started thinking about his great-grandfather Karl. Karl had completed numerous walks before dying in a 1978 stunt. Nik wanted to honor Karl's memory.

Nik stayed calm. He had an earpiece and a microphone. This allowed him to communicate with his father and TV broadcasters.

Approximately 150,000 gallons (568,000 L) of water flow over ▶ Niagara Falls every second.

As he continued his walk across the cable, he was able to share with TV viewers just how difficult it was to handle the swirling mist and wind.

After 22 minutes on the cable, the end was only a few hundred feet away. Nik was mentally and physically drained. Battling the wind had used up his energy. His hands started to go numb against the cold balancing bar he carried.

The crowd waiting at the finish line started to cheer. Their support inspired Nik. He stopped and dropped to one knee, balancing on the cable. He pumped his right fist in the air. He knew he was minutes away from history.

Right, left, right, left. Nik was just a few steps from glory. A smile broke out across his face. He ran the last few feet of the cable before sitting on it and pumping his fist triumphantly. He had just become the first person to tightrope walk over Niagara Falls.

◀ **Many tightrope walkers also perform on slacklines, which do not have as much tension as tightropes.**

Chapter 5

THE MAKING OF EVEL KNIEVEL

It was New Year's Eve in 1967. Hundreds of onlookers gathered at Caesars Palace casino in Las Vegas, Nevada. The crowd buzzed with anticipation. They were there to see Evel Knievel.

Knievel would become one of the most popular stunt performers of all time. But in 1967, he was still trying to become famous. He knew he had to make a splash to hit the big time.

So he decided to jump over the famous Caesars Palace fountains on his motorcycle. The jump was 151 feet (46 m) long. Knievel had never attempted that distance before.

The crowd's anticipation grew. Knievel was a showman. So he played to his strengths. He popped a **wheelie** in front of the crowd to increase the excitement. Then he took a few practice runs. He made sure he could get up to speed and warmed up the motorcycle without actually going off the ramp.

◄ **Evel Knievel revs his engine as he gets ready to perform a jump.**

Knievel was ready to become a household name. He gunned the engine. It buzzed loudly. He hit the ramp and took off. He flew through the air, the sunny sky providing a perfect backdrop for the cameras filming him. Knievel had hired a director and his wife to film the event. A television station said it would buy the footage if the jump turned out to be spectacular.

The crowd watched as he glided over the fountains. Knievel stood on his motorcycle's pegs. He leaned the bike back to position it for the landing ramp. But the landing was not right.

Knievel did not have enough air. His back tire landed on the ramp. But the shock of the landing caused Knievel to bounce up from the bike. His hands ripped from the handlebars.

Now Knievel had no control. The bike tires wobbled and skidded left and right. Knievel flew over the top of his handlebars, arms and legs outstretched. He flipped, landed on the hard asphalt of the casino parking lot, and continued to tumble. The crowd gasped in shock.

Knievel was rushed to a nearby hospital. He had a crushed pelvis, along with fractures in his leg, wrist, hip, and ankle. He also had a serious concussion. It kept him in a coma in the hospital for 29 days.

A good helmet is an important piece of safety gear for ▶ motorcycle stunts.

▲ Evel Knievel inspired a new generation of motorcycle-riding stunt performers.

Knievel could easily have died. But he survived, and now he was more popular than ever. He made his next jump only four months later. Venues and TV broadcasters started paying him $25,000 per performance. After the crazy Caesars Palace stunt, fans couldn't wait to see what he would attempt next.

The daredevil was a superstar of the 1960s and 1970s. He suffered more than 400 bone fractures during his career. Knievel rode his motorcycle over vehicles and pits full of dangerous animals. He even tried to use a rocket-powered motorcycle to jump over a canyon.

Knievel showed people the best and worst of life as a stunt performer. Stunt performers accomplish amazing feats to thrill crowds. But they are always one mistake away from disaster.

THINK ABOUT IT

- What do you think the best and worst parts of being a stunt performer would be?
- What kinds of stunts do you think would be your best? Why?
- Do you think stunt performers should be required to take safety measures? Why or why not?

GLOSSARY

extras (EK-struhz): Extras are people who play minor roles, often in the background. The extras on the set of *Police Story* watched as Jackie Chan performed his stunts.

friction (FRICK-shun): Friction is the rubbing of one thing against another. Jackie Chan suffered burns from the friction between his hands and the pole he slid down.

fulcrum (FUHL-krum): A fulcrum is a point of support and place for movement. Shauna Duggins used the car's steering wheel as a fulcrum so she could apply pressure to the door and escape.

green screen (GREEN SKREEN): A green screen is a background that allows directors to add special effects after filming is done. Jackie Chan started using a green screen instead of doing all of his own stunts.

stunt coordinators (STUNT koh-OR-di-nay-terz): Stunt coordinators decide which stunt performers to hire and help plan stunts. Stunt performers place their trust in stunt coordinators to set up performances correctly.

stunt double (STUNT DUB-ul): A stunt double is a person who perform stunts for actors. A stunt doubles performs dangerous acts so traditional actors don't have to.

wheelie (WEE-lee): To perform a wheelie, a person rides a motorcycle on its back tire. Evel Knievel performed a wheelie to get the crowd excited before his jump.

TO LEARN MORE

Books

Cohn, Jessica. *Fearless! Stunt People*. Huntington Beach, CA: Teacher Created Materials, 2013.

Thomas, William David. *Movie Stunt Worker*. New York: Marshall Cavendish Benchmark, 2010.

Wood, Alix. *Stunt Performer*. New York: PowerKids Press, 2014.

Web Sites

Visit our Web site for links about stunt performers: childsworld.com/links

Note to Parents, Teachers, and Librarians: We routinely verify our Web links to make sure they are safe and active sites. So encourage your readers to check them out!

SELECTED BIBLIOGRAPHY

"Daredevil Completes Walk across Niagara Falls." *CNN*. Cable News Network, 16 June 2012. Web. 13 June 2016.

Gregory, Mollie. *Stuntwomen: The Untold Hollywood Story*. Lexington, KY. University Press of Kentucky, 2015.

"The Man: Legendary Evel." *Evel Knievel*. Evel Knievel, n.d. Web. 13 June 2016.

INDEX

ABOUT THE AUTHOR

Alex Monnig is a freelance journalist from St. Louis, Missouri, who now lives in Sydney, Australia. He graduated with his master's degree from the University of Missouri in 2010. During his career he has spent time covering sporting events around the world and has written more than a dozen children's books.